97

E
OCH   Ochs, Carol
           Partridge.
             When I'm alone

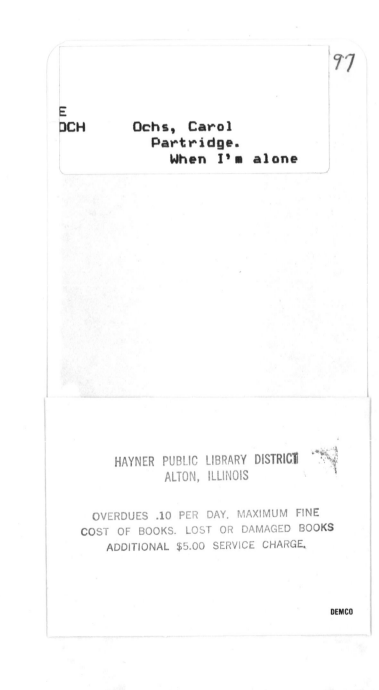

When I'm Alone

by
Carol Partridge Ochs
Illustrated by
Vicki Jo Redenbaugh

Carolrhoda Books, Inc.
Minneapolis

To Margaret, Rory,
Lee and Mary-Jo,
with thanks

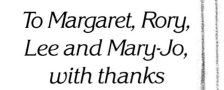

Library of Congress
Cataloging-in-Publication Data

Ochs, Carol Partridge.
    When I'm alone / by
Carol Partridge Ochs; illustrated by
Vicki Jo Redenbaugh.
        p.   cm.

    Summary: A little girl tries to explain
that it was an assortment of animals —
from ten aardvarks to one kitten — that
made the mess for which she is blamed.
    ISBN 0-87614-752-X
    [1. Cleanliness — Fiction.
2. Imagination — Fiction. 3. Animals —
Fiction. 4. Counting. 5. Stories in
rhyme.] I. Redenbaugh, Vicki Jo, ill.
II. Title.
PZ8.3.O26 Wh   1993
[E] — dc20
                        93-6348
                        CIP
                        AC

Manufactured in the
United States of America
1 2 3 4 5 6 98 97 96 95 94 93

When I'm alone, with only me,
And no one's here to disagree,
That's when the strangest things I see
And wonder, Can they really be?

It's enough to make me groan
What happens when I'm here alone.

Such troublemakers
I have known,
Those beasts
who come here
on their own.

My mother thinks
I make the mess
They leave behind.
Yes, that's her guess.

"It's not *my* doing,"
I protest,
"It's those
troublemaking pests!"

I saw ten aardvarks
   in my food,
And their behavior
   was *awfully* rude.
It put me
   in a grumpy mood
Having ten rowdy aardvarks
   in my food.

Those slurping aardvarks
   made me shudder –
Gobbling up
   my peanut butter.
As they licked their snouts,
   I heard them mutter,
"*We* won't clean up
   all this clutter."

Nine lions crowded
into my bed,
Wrinkling it up
from foot to head.

"Why don't you sleep
in the park instead?"
I yelled at nine lions
stretched out on my bed.

One lion slowly
raised his paw
And scratched his large
and furry jaw.

At me,
   he pointed one sharp claw,
Then yawned
   and gave a loud guffaw.

I found eight turtles in my tub
Giving each other's back a rub.
Tell me, Could I begin to scrub
With eight soapy turtles in my tub?

I reached right in
and pulled the plug.
Out ran the water —
glug, glug, glug.
Each turtle gave
a little shrug
And dried off on
our new bath rug.

Then seven camels found my door.
Only seven, and not one more.
Well, surely I could not ignore
Seven camels snooping at my door.

They trampled on my mother's roses
And smudged the windows with their noses.
One tangled up the garden hoses.
What *problems* a herd
   of camels poses!

Six tree frogs leaped upon my wall.
I hardly noticed them there at all
Except when they began to crawl,
Six creeping tree frogs on my wall.

Across the hall I saw them climb,
Making trails of sticky slime.
Each footstep left a gooey shine.
Who will wash up
all their grime?

I caught five goldfish in my shoe.
Can you believe the shoe was new?
I couldn't decide just what to do
With five slippery goldfish in my shoe.

The goldfish swam and splashed about
Until my shoe was wet throughout.
"You've wrecked my shoe,"
they heard me shout,
"Go back to your bowl
and don't get out!"

I saw four cows come down my street
Looking for some cow-sized seats,
And all of them had tired feet,
The four wandering cows there in my street.

They came inside
   and tried a chair.
Two sank down here;
   two plopped down there.
When they got up,
   they didn't care
That every seat
   was thick with hair.

I spied three hippos
   in my clothes;
I wonder why my clothes
   they chose.
How they got there,
   heaven knows,
Those three fat hippos
   in my clothes.

They tossed around
   my underwear
And lost a sock
   from every pair.
My bedroom made me
   stop and stare —
A horrid mess
   they'd left in there!

Two monkeys rummaged
   in my toys.
They were making *so* much noise
I knew they couldn't be
   girls or boys,
But two meddling monkeys
   in my toys.

They took apart my new airplane
And bent the tracking for my train.
"Watch what you're doing!" I complained;
Yet they kept on playing unrestrained.

I saw a kitten beneath my chair.
You think I'm joking?
    That's not fair,
Because that kitten
    was really there,
One purring kitten
        beneath my chair.

He lay curled up throughout the day
And never once got up to play.
That kitten was the only one today
Who didn't put trouble in my way.

My mother came up
from her study
and took a peek.
"What happened here?"
I heard her shriek.
"It's not *my* fault,"
I bravely said,
But my mother slowly
shook her head.

I looked around, but to my despair
They all had vanished into thin air.
Gone were the animals,
    away they'd sneaked,
Except for the kitten . . .

                who was
                    fast asleep.